Walks around Cleveland

compiled by
STUART WHITE
on behalf of
TEESSIDE TREKKERS

Dalesman Books
1985

The Dalesman Publishing Company Ltd.,
Clapham, via Lancaster LA2 8EB
First published 1985
© Stuart White, 1985

ISBN: 0 85206 828 X

Printed in Great Britain by Fretwell & Brian Ltd.,
Healey Works, Goulbourne Street, Keighley, West Yorkshire

Contents

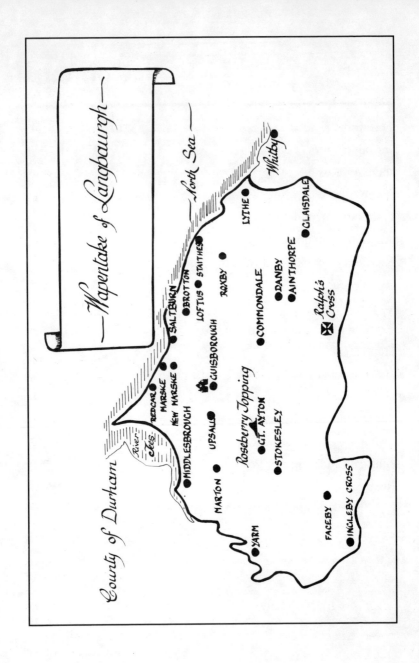

Foreword

THE geographical area encompassed by these chapters is ancient Cleveland, as opposed to the present county created by government legislation. Walking within the area ranges from sections of the 96 miles of the Cleveland Way, walked easily in a week's holiday, part of the Lyke Wake Walk, usually taking from twelve to 24 hours, down to unplanned ambles along country lanes or across fields.

This book is intended for those who wish to enjoy the countryside in short, reasonably easy rambles, whilst following rights-of-way which our forefathers have left as our heritage. The country dweller, whose land, with its stock and crops, is the source of his livelihood, should not be inconvenienced in any way by our presence. The routes described provide the knowledge to tread in places where the countryman can, and does, welcome you and bid you good-day as you pass by.

The area covered originates from the Saxon distribution of land, when the Wapentake of Langbaurgh was created. This later became known as Cleveland. The distribution of land by King Arthur was based on counties, ridings, wapentakes and tythings. Each county, irrespective of size, was divided into thirds or ridings, a name which only persists in Yorkshire. The wapentakes and tythings were more precisely defined. A wapentake, headed by a governor, consisted of ten tythings, each headed by a decurio; each tything contained ten family groups, each with its own master. The fact that there were only 100 family groups living in such a large area as ancient Cleveland does seem rather startling.

The derivation of the name Cleveland is given by William Camden, the antiquary, in translations from *Britannia* as "evidently from Cliff land, because of the many precipices and steep hills which are called cliffs, which abound in the area". The opinion of William Baxter, in *Glossarium Antiquitatum Britannicarum*, is that the name derives not from cliff, but from clay, as descriptive of the area's soil. Quotations include "in the vale and lower lands of Cleveland, a fertile clay generally prevails, although in the east and towards the coast, the soil is more barren, being chiefly a stiff, red clay". Whichever is the true origin, "Cliff land" is so characteristic of the landscape that it must be the most attractive proposition.

Gordon Lloyd

5

Introduction

THE walks described herein have been taken from the evening programme of the Teesside Trekkers, an informal group conceived and organised by Stuart White, an enthusiastic walker and scrambler. Originally from Hull, Stuart moved to Cleveland in September 1979. The group arranges about 50 walks throughout the year. Each is planned, reconnoitered and led by individual Trekkers. Our success since the inaugural walk in May 1981 is due to the support given by all members.

Whilst enjoying these walks we have found friends of quite diverse personalities and interests. One person's knowledge of birds helps us to see the dipper, diving off the rocks into the fast flowing stream, or the lapwing's nest, complete with eggs, close to the pathway. Another's interest in history brings alive the pack-horse routes, paved ways and monks trods. A geological expert describes how glacial erosion has sculpted much of the area we now know as Cleveland.

The walks are arranged, as far as is practical, in an east– west sequence and each can be completed in two to three hours in the afternoon or on a summer evening. There are woodland walks, scented by wild flowers during the spring, or with the colourful shades of autumn, to Handale Abbey or through Arncliff Woods. Evidence of Bronze Age settlers may be found on Danby Rigg or Hob on the Hill. Mining has been extensive throughout Cleveland; areas visited include the ironstone mines on Eston Moor, coal pits near Poverty Hill and alum and jet along the coast near Goldsborough.

All the walks are circular and are based on a suitable refreshment facility. Cars may be parked safely. All starting points, except Roxby, may be reached by public transport. Even so, it is as wise to check that food will be served, or buses are available, on the day required, as it is to wear stout footwear and tell someone where you are going, particularly if you are walking alone.

This book has been compiled and produced by Stuart White with walks also being contributed by Loz Howard, Barrie Metcalfe and Tony Oliver. Sketches are by Joyce Lawrence and sketch maps by Barrie Metcalfe. Our typists were Hazel Lawrence, Brenda Oliver, Rosemary Thomas and Jackie Gibson.

Ordnance Survey maps of the area include the North York Moors Tourist Map, scale one-inch to one mile, and the 1:25000 Outdoor Leisure Maps, North York Moors, East Sheet and West Sheet.

Public transport is provided by United Automobile Services, telephone Middlesbrough 224021, who cover all walks except Glaisdale and Roxby. Services to Danby, Ainthorpe and Commondale are on Saturdays only.

British Rail, telephone Middlesbrough 243208. The Middlesbrough–Whitby line serves Great Ayton, Commondale, Danby, Ainthorpe and Glaisdale.

Cleveland Transit, telephone Middlesbrough 248411, cover New Marske, Brotton, Loftus, Guisborough and Great Ayton.

Both road companies also offer various inter-village services.

Gordon Lloyd

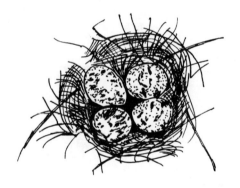

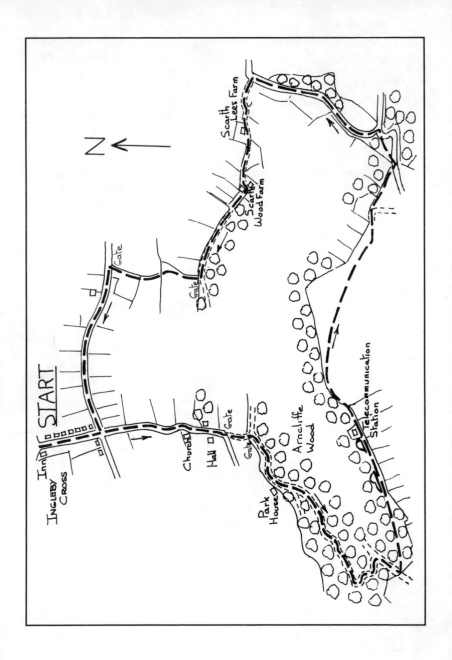

Ingleby Cross

Starting point: The Blue Bell Inn, Ingleby Cross, G.R. 449006: the inn is residential and offers a comprehensive range of bar snacks and bar meals.

Ingleby Cross comprises a small cluster of houses situated northwest of the A172. The most prominent features of the immediate vicinity are Arncliffe Hall and church. The Hall was designed by John Carr, a Georgian architect from York, and built in 1754. The church of All Saints is Norman in origin but was rebuilt in 1821 and restored in 1951. It contains a number of interesting items including a three decker pulpit and two male effigies of the Colvilles, who owned the estate during the early part of this century. In the churchyard is an area reserved for manorial family tombs.

Approximately 1½ miles south is Mount Grace Priory; founded in 1398, it is the best preserved Carthusian monastery in the country. The monks occupied individual cells in almost total isolation. It is open to the public from March to October.

Route: From the inn cross the main road, then keep ahead along the lane, passing the church and hall, until reaching a signposted footpath on the left. Follow this path to the bottom of Arncliffe Wood before turning right along the main forest road. This road climbs and twists uphill, past Park House, until reaching a boundary gate. The route now continues by way of a much narrower path leading off to the left. When the path levels off, bear left past two small disused quarries to reach a telecommunications station. This station occupies the summit of the Arncliffe, a rocky nab on the wooded hillside. Continue ahead, alongside the wall, then turn right across a field corner to emerge on to open moor. Immediately to the left is an old boundary stone.

Where the path forks bear left. The view ahead encompasses Whorl Hill, Carlton Bank and Coalmire. Follow the path as it descends to the right of enclosed forestry and grazing land to reach the road. After crossing a cattle grid turn immediately left, above a small beck, then, at the road, head towards Potto. When the road bends sharply to the right follow the track passing to the left of Scarth Lees Farm. Continue through the field gate and along the right-hand field boundary to reach Scarth Wood Farm. The path passes between the buildings before swinging right into an enclosed lane. Keep ahead as the path crosses rough grassland and into the wood. Where the grass path obviously widens and bends left, turn right through a field gate. Follow the boundary of three fields to reach the road, which should then be followed to Ingleby Cross.

Distance: 6 miles.

Martin eNeil

Faceby and Whorlton

Starting point: Sutton Arms, Faceby, G.R. 496032: the inn offers light snacks, with a wider selection of bar meals being available each Wednesday and Friday evening.

Whorlton, with its ruined church and castle, is of historical interest. The church of Holy Cross dates from the twelfth century. Remaining from the original building is the chancel arch and part of the north arcade, the south arcade being added in about 1200 and the tower approximately 200 years later. The Meynell tomb, the Meynells were once landowners in the area, is situated in the chancel. It is surmounted by a crocketed canopy covering a hollow oak effigy, c1305–10, reputedly of Sir Nicholas de Meynell. The castle, a motte and bailey type, occupies a strong defensive site. It was built during the reign of Richard II and has seen many owners, including the Meynells. Their coat-of-arms is to be found above the gateway, along with those of the D'Arcys and the Grays. The present tower house was erected in about 1400. At that time the motte was reduced and the original buildings became less important.

Route: From the Sutton Arms follow the road signposted "Faceby Only", until the first turning right. After passing the village church veer left between two stone pillars, then diagonally right to the corner of Whorl Hill Wood. Climb the stile, then follow the path round the bottom of the wood and past Whorl Hill Farm. After passing through a large metal gate keep ahead alongside the hedge at the top of rough pasture. The path eventually crosses a stile into a cultivated field, then bears diagonally right over grazing land to emerge in Whorlton. To explore the church and castle follow the road ahead.

The walking route turns left along the lane to Whorlton House then joins a wide farm track leading straight ahead to Perish Crook. Pass to the left of the boundary fence, through a large gate, then along the hedgeside to a second gate. Follow the path round the field boundary to reach Huthwaite Green. Turn left, then left again just past the telephone box, on to the Cleveland Way path. Where the path ascends steeply to the right, keep ahead through a small gate before entering Faceby Plantation by a second gate. Bear left,

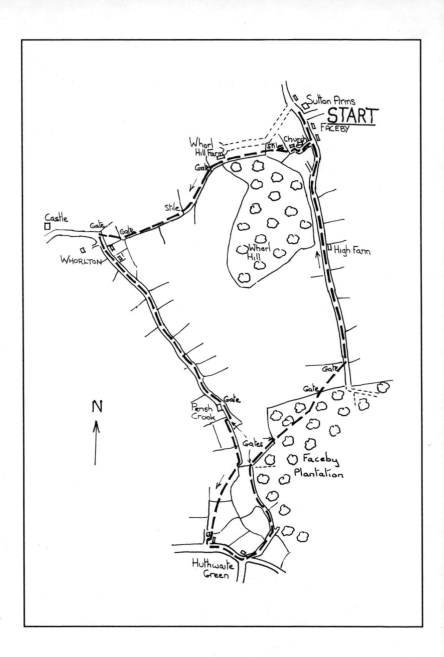

Sutton Arms
START
FACEBY
Whorl Hill Farm
Stile
Church
Gate
Stile
Castle
Gate
Gate
WHORLTON
Whorl Hill
High Farm
N
Gate
Gate
Gate
Pensh Crook
Gates
Faceby Plantation
Huthwaite Green

then continue through the plantation to emerge eventually into open grazing land. Cross the field diagonally to the right and out into the lane. Ahead is Carlton Bank, rising to a height of 1,338 feet. Turn left to return to Faceby.

Distance: 5 miles.

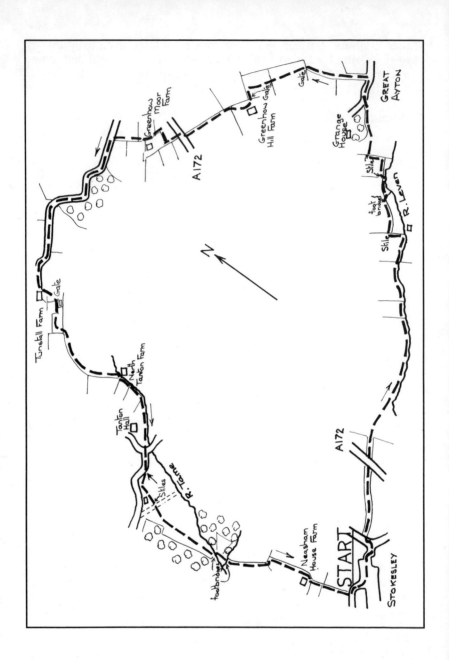

Stokesley Circular

Starting point: Market Place, Stokesley, G.R. 526086: within the Market Place is a variety of refreshment facilities, including the Cafe Royal; the Angel Inn and Golden Lion Inn offer morning coffee, bar meals and have a separate restaurant whilst the Queens Head serves light snacks.

Stokesley is a typical market town and has been declared a Conservation Area. There are a number of interesting historical aspects to the town, including a seventeenth century bridge across the River Leven, the parish church of St. Peter, dating back to the fifteenth century, Stone Hall in the High Street, Georgian houses and indication of past industry. Each feature is small in itself but Stokesley's collective history makes it worthy of exploration.

The Rivers Leven and Tame, which form the basis of this walk, are, in reality, little more than becks. The former meanders through Great Ayton, Stokesley and Hutton Rudby before turning north to enter the River Tees east of Yarm, whilst the latter's source is south of Nunthorpe. It then flows to the west of Stokesley before entering the River Leven at Leven Mouth, south-west of the town.

Route: Leave the Market Place by following the road in an almost easterly direction towards a small roundabout. Turn left, then after approximately 50 yards, right along a fenced path passing an agricultural machinery manufacturers. Follow this path to the A172, cross the road and enter the field opposite.

At this point there is the first view of the surrounding hills. Immediately ahead is Roseberry Topping, at 1,051 feet perhaps the area's most outstanding geographical feature: to its right Captain Cook's Monument surmounts Easby Moor. To your right are the rolling Cleveland Hills over which pass the Lyke Wake Walk and the Cleveland Way, two long distance footpaths.

A distinct path continues ahead and then follows the north bank of the River Leven, as far as a light industrial factory on the opposite side. The route now turns left along the hedgeside for approximately 100 yards, then right over a stile. Keeping the hedge on the right follow the path ahead, cross a footbridge, then rejoin the riverside path. After a stile follow the field boundary round to the left to reach another stile by a large wooden post. Continue ahead past Grange House to emerge eventually on to Yarm Lane. Proceed in the direction of Great Ayton. After a short distance turn left, between the buildings, on to a signposted bridleway, which leads directly ahead before turning left to reach Greenhow Hill Farm. Take the farm road down to the main road, known locally as Pannierman Lane, and cross to a continuation of the bridleway slightly to the right. Follow the route around the boundary of Greenhow Moor Farm to join Green Lane. Turn left towards the small farmstead of Tunstall, a distance of nearly one mile, then follow the broad path in the direction of Tunstall Cottage. Shortly before the cottage, turn right through a field gate. Continue by keeping close to the left-hand boundary, pass into the next field through a gap between the hedge and fence, then maintain a central course before veering left at the drainage gutter to climb the wooden fence obstructing the gateway.

The path now follows the course of this gutter until it flows into the River Tame near North Tanton Farm. Shortly before the junction turn right over a wooden bridge, immediately left along the field boundary, then follow a broad path to the farm road. Pass through the gate opposite to follow the River Tame as far as Tanton Hall, where the path meets the road via a flight of steps and a stile near the bridge. After crossing the road continue in the direction of Seamer until reaching the "Public Footpath Stokesley" sign. Bear right down the middle of the field, across a farm road, then directly ahead aiming for the gap between two small woods. Negotiate a stile before again following the River Tame, which is crossed by a footbridge, to emerge into a clearing. Turn right, cross the left-hand of two footbridges, then, keeping the boundary fence on the left, continue ahead to enter the hedged lane leading to Neasham House Farm. After passing to the left of the buildings continue ahead, along the access road, finally to regain the Market Place by turning left along the street.

Distance: 7 miles.

Airy Holme and Low Easby

Starting point: Royal Oak Hotel, High Street, Great Ayton, G.R. 563107: the hotel is residential and offers a range of bar meals, luncheons and evening dinners.

Great Ayton has strong associations with the explorer, Captain James Cook. He was born three miles away at Marton in 1728. His father then obtained employment at Airy Holme Farm which led to James attending the local Postgate School for five years from 1736. The schoolroom now houses a small Cook Museum. After leaving school, James worked with his father for two years before moving to Staithes, where he worked as a grocer before embarking on a sea-going career. Also in Great Ayton is an obelisk, marking the site of Captain Cook's parents' retirement cottage, which was dismantled and removed to Melbourne, Australia, in 1934. The grave of his mother, and five of his brothers and sisters, is to be found in All Saints' Churchyard. Approximately two miles away a monument to the explorer surmounts Easby Moor which, at 1,064 feet, is deceptively higher than its neighbour, Roseberry Topping. It takes the form of an obelisk, is 51 feet high and was erected in 1827. Captain Cook was killed in Hawaii in 1779.

Route: Leave the High Street in an easterly direction, to pass the John Pease Cottages, before turning right through an iron gate. Keep ahead along the distinct path, passing Cleveland Lodge on the left and with a clear view of Easby Moor to the right. This path eventually crosses the Esk Valley railway, running from Middlesbrough to Whitby, then continues along the fence to enter Cliff Ridge Wood by a stile in the field corner. After passing through an iron gate, turn right to join a path bearing diagonally uphill. Along this path are fine views of the Cleveland Hills and Great Ayton.

At the top of the wood maintain the diagonal course over the field to Airy Holme Farm. The landscape is now dominated by Roseberry Topping, 1,051 feet high. Continue by keeping left of the farm to join the metalled road and eventually cross Dikes Lane. Shortly after the crossroads turn right on to a wide, rough track which should be followed to the outskirts of Little Ayton. Bear left before the first building, past a detached house, then keep alongside

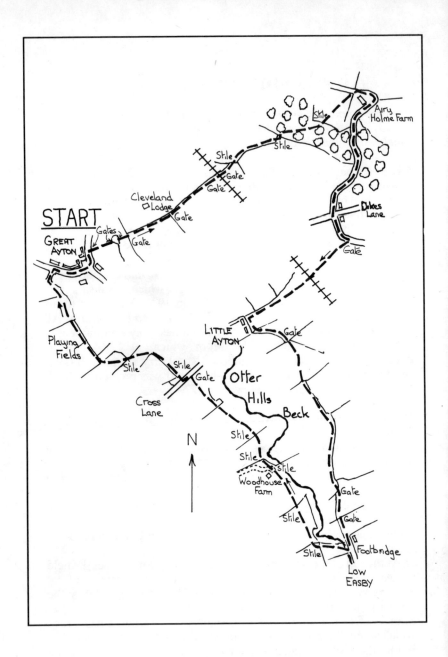

START

GREAT AYTON

Gates

Gate

Cleveland Lodge

Gate

Gate

Gate

Stile

Stile

Stile

Stile

Airy Holme Farm

Dikes Lane

Gate

Playing Fields

LITTLE AYTON

Gate

Otter Hills

Beck

Stile

Stile

Gate

Cross Lane

N

Stile

Stile

Woodhouse Farm

Stile

Stile

Gate

Gate

Stile

Stile

Footbridge

Low EASBY

the hedge to join a grass path across cultivated fields towards Low Easby. On the edge of the village turn right over a humped bridge crossing Otter Hills Beck. Continue ahead to cross a stile to the right of a field gate, then along the side of the fence and across the pasture to Woodhouse Farm.

Pass to the right of the farm, and out on to the access road, before bearing right again, over a stile, to follow the field boundary anti-clockwise to a further stile. Now keep ahead, with the beck below, to reach Cross Lane. Turn left for approximately 30 yards, then right over a stile in the hedge. Continue by the right side of the fence opposite, bear diagonally left, then right along field boundaries, with sports fields to either side, finally to re-enter Great Ayton. Turn right to the starting point.

Distance: 5 miles.

Roseberry Topping and Hanging Stone

Starting point: Kings Head Hotel, Newton-under-Roseberry, G.R. 571130: the hotel offers a range of bar snacks and bar meals.

Roseberry Topping stands in isolation on the western edge of the Cleveland Hills. Rising to a height of 1,051 feet, it has the shape and character of much higher peaks. Over the years the hill's name has varied: in the twelfth century it was Othensberg, in 1231 Onesberg, and, by the sixteenth century, Osburye Toppyne. Mining has taken place in the vicinity. In the seventeenth and eighteenth centuries alum was quarried for use in the textile and tanning industries, followed by jet in the Victorian era and ironstone in the 1920s. Such operations have scarred the upper slopes but the steep climb to the summit is rewarded by the views of the Cleveland Hills and across Teesside to the sea.

Hanging Stone is the predominant feature of Royston Scar, from which may be seen to the east (right) Highcliff Nab and, to the north-west, Eston Moor. Ahead is the town of Guisborough and beyond, the coast.

Roseberry Topping

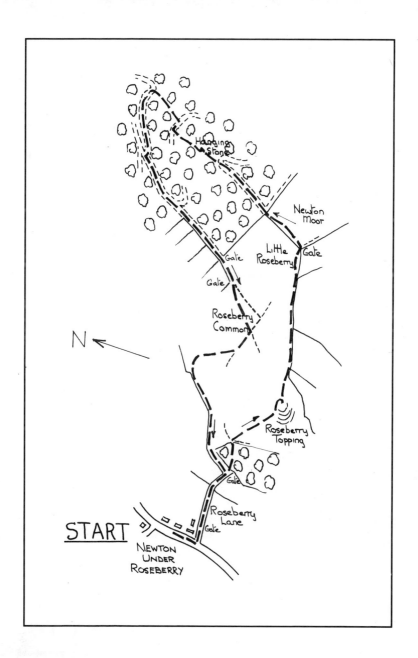

N ←

Hanging Stone

Newton Moor

Little Roseberry

Gate

Gate

Gate

Roseberry Common

Roseberry Topping

Gate

START

Roseberry Lane

Gate

NEWTON UNDER ROSEBERRY

Route: From the hotel turn left past a row of stone cottages, then left again into Roseberry Lane. Follow the lane to Newton Wood and up the stepped path before bearing left to the edge of the trees. To reach the summit turn sharp right along the distinct path. The descent is down the east face to the col but only to rise again past Little Roseberry on to Newton Moor. After passing through a wooden gate, bear left over the moor to enter Hanging Stone Wood by a stile to the left of a gate. Continue straight ahead along Royston Bank. Where the forest track makes a hairpin bend to the right, keep ahead along a narrow path leading to Hanging Stone. After enjoying the view, maintain a downhill course to reach another forest track. Turn right for approximately 30 yards, then left, eventually to reach a rough grass track. Turn left. At the main junction bear left again. Keep ahead until this track starts to climb, then take the grass track to the right; pass through a wooden gate finally to reach a larger gate opening on to Roseberry Common. Follow the right-hand fork. At two subsequent forks bear right to descend round the base of Roseberry Topping and re-enter the lane.

Distance: 4 miles.

Eston Moor

Starting point: Cross Keys Hotel, Upsall, near Guisborough, G.R. 567158: the hotel offers bar meals, selectable from a hot and cold buffet, together with full restaurant facilities. There is also a beer garden with children's play area.

Eston Moor rises to a height of 793 feet and is the most northerly of the Cleveland moors. On the Nab, a rocky promontory overlooking the Tees Valley and the highest point of the moor, is the site of a Bronze Age Hill Fort. The ditch and rampart still survive, enclosing an area of about 2½ acres. With the cliffs providing a natural defence to the north-west an impression can be gained of its formidable defensive structure. Excavations this century suggest that the fort was still occupied in the early Iron Age. The stone column was constructed in 1956 from the remains of a Napoleonic beacon tower.

The north-west face of the moor is the site of the old Eston ironstone mines, the largest and most productive of all the Cleveland mines. In operation from 1850, a total of over 163 million tons of ironstone was produced in its 99 year history. Founded by John Vaughan, their success proved to be the basis for the iron and steel industry on Teesside. Careful exploration of the area reveals many remains including haulage engine houses, overgrown drift entrances, the powder magazine and a ventilation fan house.

Route: Turn left out of the car park and approximately 30 yards beyond the hotel cross a stile on the left. Follow the path directly ahead along the boundary of the fields to reach eventually a broad track by a farm gate. Turn right and continue eastwards, past a small plantation, before swinging left after crossing a stile by a farm gate. The distinct path eventually passes to the left of the visible remains of a disused ironstone mine and dips into a hollow. Past the gorse-covered spoil heap bear right on to a narrow path and, ignoring all tracks branching left, cross the moorland finally to reach Eston Nab. Here, there are extensive views of the sharply contrasting urban expanse of Middlesbrough, the industrial sprawl of I.C.I. and beyond to the Tees Docks and Hartlepool. To the north-east are the resorts of Redcar, Marske and Saltburn, flanking the North Sea.

From the Nab re-trace the same path for a short distance, before

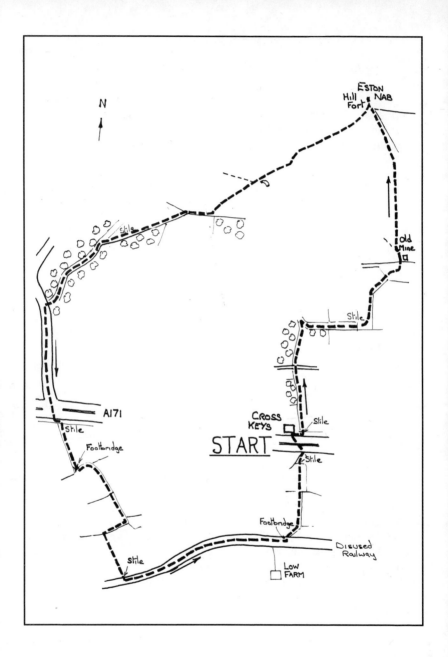

N

ESTON NAB

Hill Fort

Old Mine

Stile

Stile

A171

Stile

Footbridge

Stile

CROSS KEYS

START

Stile

Stile

Footbridge

Disused Railway

Low FARM

bearing right by the settlement fortification, on to a wide grassy path. Again taking care to ignore all branch tracks, follow this path over Eston Moor. Shortly after passing a small pond take the left fork and eventually bear right on to the downhill path, with first farmland, then woodland, to the left. At the bottom cross the stile and bear left along the lower part of Ten Acre Bank to reach the metalled road. Follow the road downhill, cross the dual carriageway, then turn left for approximately 40 yards, before joining a footpath signposted "Newton 1½ miles". After crossing a footbridge, bear left along the boundary of two fields and then right where this path meets an obvious field track. It is now necessary to look out for a yellow waymarker painted on the trunk of a hawthorn tree. At this point turn sharp left across the field, to locate a stile in the fence opposite, then bear left along the disused railway, as far as a point opposite Low Farm, clearly visible on the right. Cross the footbridge, then follow the path through the fields to emerge opposite the starting point.

Distance: 6 miles.

Guisborough

Starting point: Market Place, Guisborough, G.R. 614160: the town, with its various restaurants, cafes and inns, all within a small area, offers refreshment facilities to satisfy all tastes and occasions.

Guisborough, considered to be the capital of ancient Cleveland, has been a market town since 1263. In recent years it has expanded into a dormitory town for Teesside, with a population of about 20,000 inhabitants. The Priory was founded in 1119, by Robert de Brus, for the rich Augustinian Order, and dedicated to St. Mary. Although suffering financial troubles, it was found to be one of the country's richest priories when dissolved by Henry VIII in the 1530s. Its ruins are dominated by the east wall, rising to a height of almost 100 feet. Next to the Priory is the parish church of St. Nicholas. Originally built over 400 years ago, it was modernised in 1794, then restored to its original Perpendicular style early this century. The market cross is of Georgian design. Guisborough has also been an important mining area. Alum quarries were worked in the period around 1606 whilst ironstone was mined at various locations from 1856–1931.

Route: From the market place follow the road past the market cross, then bear right on to the path running alongside the parish church. In turn this passes the Priory and the old grammar school, now a sixth form college named after the last prior, Robert Purseglove, before veering right across Applegarth. At the road turn left, then right towards Foxdale Farm. After crossing a stile on the left, follow a waymarked path, over the fields, to Little Waterfall Farm. To the left can be seen Gisborough Hall, whilst to the right is evidence of the discontinued railway. At the farm turn right. Keep ahead along the broad track leading to the top of Spa Wood, so named as a reminder of medicinal waters discovered in the 1820s but now lost.

Once past the ruined waterworks, turn right on to a path signposted "Cleveland Way". This distinct path follows the top of the wood, affording extensive views of Guisborough and the surrounding area, including Eston Moor and Upleatham Hill. The waymarked route should be maintained until it is crossed by a much narrower path. At this point descend to the lower forest path, then turn left past a disused quarry. As the path widens keep ahead, with Highcliff Nab clearly visible in the near distance. Eventually the

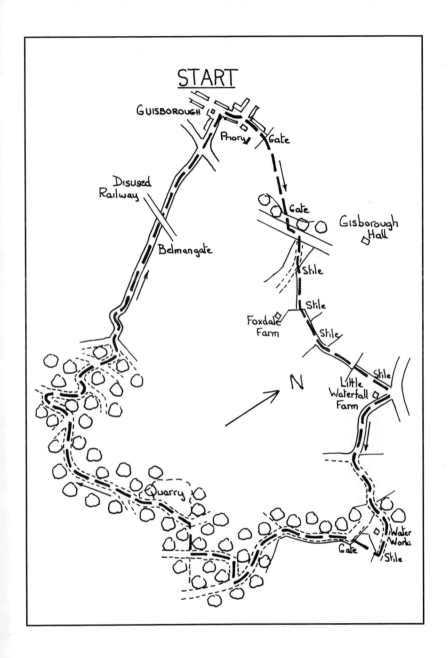

START

GUISBOROUGH

Priory · Gate

Disused Railway

Belmangate

Gate

Gisborough Hall

Stile

Stile

Foxdale Farm

Stile

Stile

Little Waterfall Farm

N

Quarry

Water Works

Gate

Stile

route swings right, downhill. This downhill course should be followed at all junctions until the edge of the forestry is reached. Pass through the gate to join the lane leading into Belmangate and the town centre.

Distance: 6 miles.

Toward Guisboro'
JL

Errington Wood and Upleatham

Starting point: Yorkshire Lass, New Marske, G.R. 622212: the hotel offers a range of bar snacks and bar meals.

New Marske appears on records dated 1205, when it was only farmland, but the discovery of Bronze Age barrows to the south of the village indicates much earlier settlement. Its development as a village community came with the nineteenth century ironstone boom. Mining continued from 1851–1923; afterwards the village fell into decline until grants became available, to improve housing and services, in the late 1950s. This was followed by an extensive housing project which expanded the community into a large dormitory village.

Errington Wood occupies the northern face of a low outlier of the Cleveland Hills. It rises to a height of almost 600 feet at which point it gives way to arable farmland and meadow.

Upleatham is a small, exclusive village occupying a sheltered position and surrounded by attractive countryside. The church of St. Andrew, situated in isolation from the village and dating back to the twelfth century, is often claimed to be the smallest church in England. Such a claim is false as the building is only a surviving part of a larger church. Within the village is a Norman church in the Revival style of 1835.

Tocketts Mill is a unique water corn mill dating back to 1715. It was opened to the public in 1983 after restoration work by the Cleveland Building Preservation Trust.

Route: From the hotel turn left, then right along Pontac Road. Where the road ends follow the broad path ahead, through an iron gate and uphill into Errington Wood. Just before a wooden seat bear left up the steep path leading to the top of the wood. At this point it is necessary to stop, not merely to regain breath, but also to absorb the industrial landscape flanking the River Tees, the Tees estuary and beyond to Hartlepool, nestling in the north-east corner of the modern county.

The walk continues by crossing the field along the left side of a hawthorn hedge, then turning right on to a broad field road as far as a large gate. Bear right along the fenced path, through the gate at the end, then downhill alongside the boundary wall to a ladder stile.

29

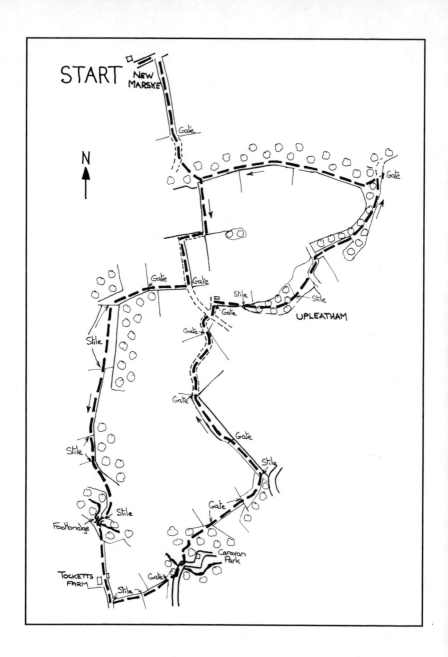

START NEW MARSKE

N

Gate

Gate

Gate   Gate

Stile   Stile

Gate

UPLEATHAM

Stile

Gate

Gate

Gate

Gate

Stile

Stile

Stile

Stile

Footbridge

Caravan Park

Gate

TOCKETTS FARM

Stile   Gate

Cross into the next field and aim for the far side, where entry is gained to a green lane by a further stile. The view ahead encompasses the town of Guisborough overlooked by the towering Highcliff, with Roseberry Topping beyond.

Once through the green lane the path enters open pasture. Continue ahead for approximately 100 yeards, bear diagonally right across the pasture, then follow Tocketts Dump Wood boundary fence to the stile in the bottom corner. Cross Tocketts Beck by the footbridge, then bear left, uphill, past a disused shaft. On emerging from the wood continue towards the farm, pass between the outbuildings and onto the access road, before crossing a stile on the left. Proceed along the left boundary of two fields, through a wooden gate, and on to the road leading to Tocketts Mill. After re-crossing the beck bear diagonally left towards the wood. Follow the right-hand path uphill through the trees until entering a field by a wooden gate. Continue along the boundary fence and over rough grassland to reach a footpath signposted "Upleatham".

Follow the distinct lane until bearing right, then left, over open pasture to reach a large barn. Pass immediately to the right of this building, and ahead along the field boundary, to enter Village Wood by a stile on the right, near the beginning of a barbed fence. As the path is followed through the wood the village of Upleatham is visible to the right. Leave Village Wood by a stile, and down some steps, before continuing ahead along a walled path. Where this path forks bear right over a rough stone stile and cross the field into Errington Wood. Follow the woodland path until the junction of four paths is reached: turn left, towards the top of the wood, and continue along this distinct path to link eventually with the outward route, which should be retraced downhill to the starting point.

Distance: 6 miles.

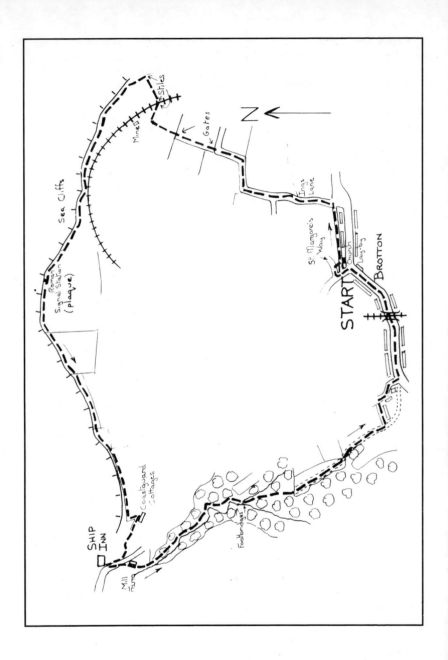

32

Huntcliff and Saltburn

Starting point: The Crown Hotel, Brotton, G.R. 687197: the hotel offers morning coffee, together with warm and cold snacks and a selection of bar meals.

Brotton, once an ironstone mining village, lies at the junction of the A173 and A174 roads from Guisborough and Middlesbrough respectively. Consequently, it is an important link in the main coast road tourist route. The Church of St. Margaret, built in the Perpendicular style, was completed in 1891. There are some interesting seventeenth and eighteenth century houses in High Street.

Saltburn is a relatively quiet resort, with a sandy beach spreading north-west to beyond Redcar. Old Saltburn, nestling beneath Huntcliff, was first recorded in 1215 when it was the site of a hermitage, later donated to Whitby Abbey. It has also been a notorious smuggling area and survived as a small fishing port until about 1860. Today, it is still a focal point for local fishermen and anglers. The Ship Inn and Ship House are about five hundred years old, whilst the pier was built in 1868 but is now only a fraction of its original length. Modern Saltburn, overlooking the beach, began to develop during the Victorian era and still retains many features of that period in its shops, houses and hotels. The wooded glens, bordering Skelton Beck, are a natural asset and incorporate the Italian Gardens, laid out approximately 120 years ago.

Route: From the hotel go uphill, turn left at the road junction, then first right into St. Margaret's Way. From the steps on the right follow the pathway, along the back of the bungalows, as far as the last row of terraced houses on the right, then turn left into Ings Lane. Follow the lane through the gate and straight ahead at the junction. At the third bend follow the path along the boundary of a large field. After passing through a gate continue ahead to a point opposite a ladder stile to your right. Cross the railway — with care — via this stile then gain the cliff top path by a further stile in the fence opposite.

To the right is the coastal village of Skinningrove, an important shipping point for ironstone when mining was at its height. The grey building across the field to the left is the remains of a mine ventilation pump. It is one of two well preserved examples in the East Cleveland area and worth exploration. The shaft entrance is clearly visible.

The walk continues by turning left and following the path along the top of Huntcliff to Saltburn; en route it passes a plaque detailing the site of a Roman signal station. After reaching the Ship Inn, cross the road and turn left along the bridleway passing to the right of Mill Farm. Past the farm fork right into a wood, previously hidden from view, to continue upstream alongside Saltburn Gill, for nearly a mile. After passing a bridge on the right and crossing a smaller bridge, bear left uphill to emerge into an open field. Follow the path along the edge of the wood and across a field to the outskirts of Brotton. Turn left along the back of the houses, right by a metal gate, then follow the road through the housing estate to the main road. Turn uphill back to the starting point.

Distance: 6 miles.

Handale Abbey

Starting point: Market Place, Loftus, G.R. 723182: within the immediate vicinity refreshments are offered by the Tea Shoppe, together with a selection of inns serving light snacks only.

Loftus, possibly of Viking origin, grew with the development of the alum industry. Mining was at its height in the seventeenth century and provided work for over 200 years. Traces of the workings are to be found on the cliffs to the north. As alum supplies dwindled ironstone was discovered and mined from 1865–1958. The population doubled and Loftus became a small town. Since that period it has grown steadily and now has a population approaching 5,000. Association with mining continues to the present day through the extraction of potash from the nearby Boulby Mine. St. Leonard's Church, although much rebuilt, retains its tower of 1811. **Handale Abbey,** now a working farm, is the site of a Benedictine priory, founded in 1133 by Richard de Percy, and dedicated to the Virgin Mary. At the time of the dissolution, in the 1530s, it housed only eight nuns. A cotton factory has also operated in the area; this was demolished in 1846.

Route: Leave the Market Place by turning down the short road, near the Post Office, leading into a narrow passageway running between the east end of the church and the Regal Cinema. At the bottom, turn right between the houses, then right again to cross a narrow stream by a footbridge. The path continues uphill, crossing the single track railway serving the potash mine at Boulby, before emerging into a field through a wooden gate. Bear left and keep to the edge of the field, with the farmstead of South Loftus on the left, until reaching a wooden kissing gate. Pass into a broad grass lane, then follow the boundary fence first left, then right and finally enter the wood by a stile.

At this point it is worth a short stop to turn and enjoy the view. Nestled midst the surrounding farmland is the long, narrow town of Loftus. To its left the smooth top and gentle slope of Warsett Hill gives way to the sheer face of Huntcliff.

Continue by following the path along the edge of the wood, cross the stream by a footbridge, then out into a field. Follow the waymarked route across the pasture, passing mixed woodland to

35

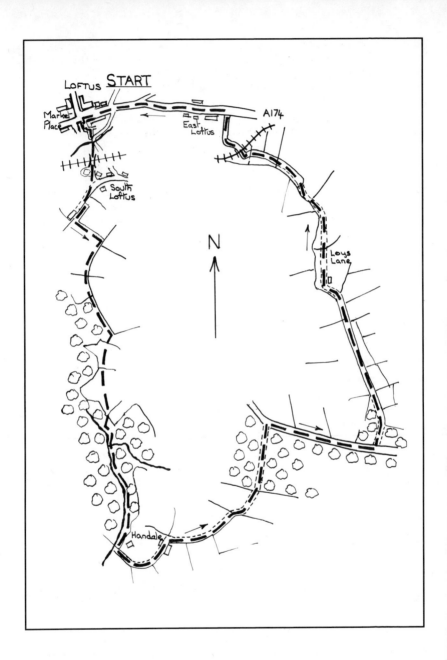

the right. At a field gate keep ahead to enter the wood by a stile in the far corner. Drop downhill, between the trees, then turn left along the beckside. After crossing a narrow tributary note the old beech tree on the right. The path follows the beck upstream, and across a farm access road, before emerging into rough pasture. At the far side enter a thicket and turn immediately uphill to join the cart track passing between the farm and outbuildings of Handale Abbey. The track continues alongside the fields and through Warren Wood, eventually to reach a minor road known as Grinkle Lane. Turn right and follow this lane until reaching a broad path on the left. This is Loys Lane. After passing through and alongside the wood, it winds its way around and between fields, to pass allotments and the cemetery, before joining the main road in East Loftus, just below the Market Place.

Distance: 5 miles.

Hob on the Hill

Starting point: The Cleveland Inn, Commondale, G.R. 663105: the inn offers morning coffee, bar snacks, grills and teas.

Commondale is a small hamlet surrounded by open moorland. Although now entirely rural, it was the scene of much industrial activity in the nineteenth century. This included a large brickworks, pottery, milling and quarrying.

Hob on the Hill, a large, possibly Bronze Age, tumulus, situated north-west of the hamlet, is one of many burial howes to be found on moorland ridges. Running south from the Hob is an earth bank with upright stones, probably boundary markers between ancient tribes or villages. A definite boundary stone is Hob Cross, bearing the date 1798, and lying at the meeting point of several old paths.

Route: With the inn to the left take the road uphill out of the village. After the last building on the right bear right along the grassy path, which eventually becomes paved, to cross the beck by a stone bridge. Follow the path climbing away from the beck, over the open moor, until its junction with a very distinct path appearing from the left. Turn right and continue ahead until reaching a row of shooting butts on the right, which should then be followed to Hob on the Hill.

For the next 1¼ miles the going becomes more difficult as there is no distinct path. It is necessary to walk through the heather and across some very wet moorland, therefore it is important to be appropriately equipped. Anyone feeling unsuited to this terrain must retrace the route to Commondale.

Those continuing should head due north across the moor, until reaching a dry stone boundary wall, then turn right along the equally indistinct bridleway from Guisborough. For a short distance this runs parallel to the wall in a due easterly direction. When the wall starts to bend away to the left the bridleway curves to the right eventually to join a much clearer paved way emerging on the left.

This is known as Quakers Causeway. Bear right to follow this old path, past the tumulus of Black Howes, until its junction with the road to Castleton. Continue ahead as far as the left-hand bend. Immediately past the chevrons bear in an almost southerly direction towards the small wood ahead. Pass to the left of the wood before following the road downhill into Commondale.

Distance: 6 miles.

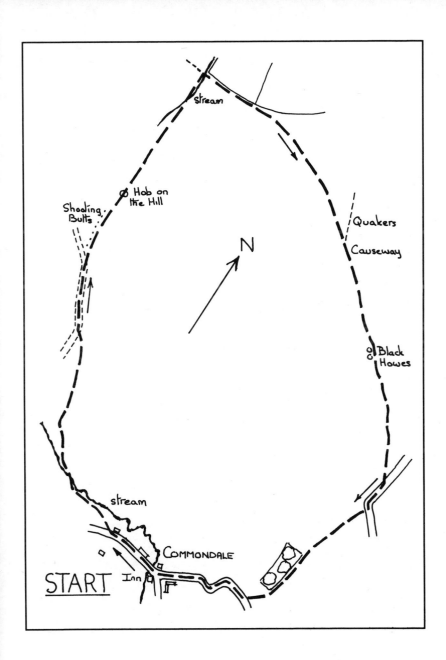

stream

Hob on the Hill

Shooting Butts

N

Quakers Causeway

Black Howes

stream

COMMONDALE

START

Inn

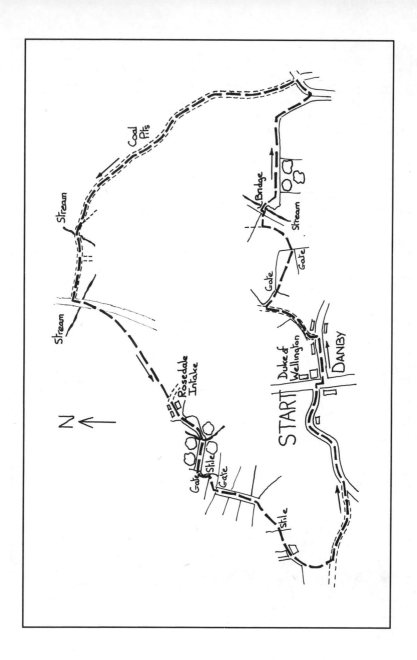

N ←

Coal Pits

Stream

Stream

Stream

Bridge

Stream

Gate

Gate

Gate

Rosedale
Intake

Gate
Stile
Gate

Stile

Duke of
Wellington

START

DANBY

Poverty Hill and Danby Low Moor

Starting point: The Duke of Wellington, Danby, G.R. 708087: the inn is residential, offering a good selection of light snacks and bar meals.

Danby is situated towards the head of the Esk Valley and immediately below Danby Low Moor. Its most interesting features, Beacon Hill, Duck Bridge and Danby Castle are to be found away from the village centre. The beacon, at 981 feet, is the highest point in the area: it is approximately two miles east and offers extensive views of the northern dales, Esk Valley and Scaling Dam. Duck Bridge is to the south-east. Of the narrow pack-horse style, it dates from about 1386 but was rebuilt in the early eighteenth century by George Duck, whose name it now carries. Close by are the remains of Danby Castle. Built in the fourteenth century, it is one of the earliest fortified houses built with angled towers set around an inner courtyard. Now a working farm, it also houses the Courtroom in which the estate Court Leet is held.

Danby Lodge, formerly a shooting lodge and now a National Park Moors Centre, is situated on the road to Lealholm. Open daily, from Easter to October, it offers a permanent interpretive exhibition, plus guided walks each Sunday during July and August. The grounds cover 13 acres of woodland, meadow and garden.

Route: Leave the village in an easterly direction, then turn left at the end of a row of terraced houses. Bear right along the track leading on to the moor, keeping a stone wall on the left. At the end of the wall continue ahead until reaching a wall corner. Then bear right, pass through a gateway, and follow the path downhill, to the bottom right-hand corner of the field. Through the gate the route goes left and downhill. Where the path forks bear right, to cross a stile and a footbridge, before following the line of the boundary wall up Poverty Hill, then round to join a metalled road. Turn uphill, then, after a short distance, left, on to a broad track. Along this track will be seen numerous mounds and pits. They date from the period 1748–1890 when coal was mined in the area. The seams were only thin, with much of the coal being used to burn lime for use in improving local farmland.

The distinct track continues ahead passing Doubting Castle, an abandoned farmhouse, before emerging on to the road. Turn left for a quarter mile, then bear south-west over rough moorland to Rosedale Intake. Pass to the right of the farmhouse, and over the field, before curving right to cross two streams, then climb uphill alongside a fence. At the top follow the wall ahead and left. After a stile bear diagonally right to enter a green lane. Where the lane ends bear diagonally right, over rough pasture, to locate a stile in the fence. Follow the path ahead as it passes between enclosures and curves downhill. Ahead is the Esk Valley, with Castleton to the right and Ainthorpe to the left. At the bottom turn left along a wide, grass path, which eventually meets the motor road leading back to Danby.

Distance: 5 miles.

Rosedale Intake.

Danby Dale and Danby Rigg

Starting point: Fox and Hounds, Ainthorpe, G.R. 704077: the inn offers a range of bar snacks and bar meals.

Ainthorpe is a small rural community where the ancient game of quoits, introduced to this country by the Romans, is still played on the village green.

Danby Dale opens into the Esk Valley from its southern side. It is approximately three miles long, bounded to the west by Castleton Rigg and to the east by Danby Rigg. Located within the dale are eighteenth century Danby Church and Botton village. The church is situated 1½ miles from the present day village; it is speculated that an earlier Danby, now "lost", existed nearby. Botton village is a community for mentally handicapped people, which was established by the Camphill Village Trust in 1955. Today, it exceeds 400 acres of farmland plus craft workshops, village square, social centre and church. Botton provides a predominently self-sufficient life-style for about 150 villagers who are assisted by a large network of co-workers.

Danby Rigg rises to a height of 1,022 feet. It is the site of one of numerous Bronze Age settlements to be found within the North York Moors.

Route: Follow the road leading out of the village. Where it passes between two telegraph poles join the grass path alongside the drystone wall, then continue in the direction of Rowan Tree Farm. Pass directly in front of the farmhouse and through the iron gate in the wall. Keep ahead along the paved path, then through a wooden gate towards the next farm. The route continues via the middle one of three gates, bears left along a walled path for a short distance, before finally emerging on to the farm road to the left of an outbuilding. Turn right past the cottage, then left when reaching the motor road. At the sharp bend keep straight ahead, with Danby church on the right, to enter the wood by a small wooden gate. The path drops steeply down to the beck, over the bridge, and along the field boundary to rejoin the motor road. Turn right along the road, as far as East Cliff, then head towards the farm. Pass to the right of the farmhouse and round the barn. Continue along the right-hand boundary of two fields, then follow the path as it curves its way

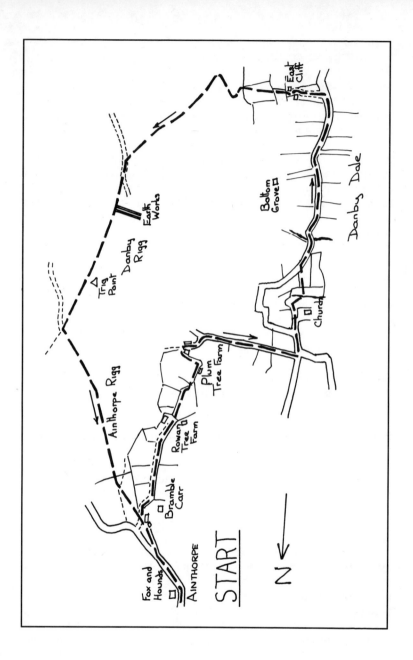

START

N

Fox and Hounds
AINTHORPE

Bramble Carr

Rowan Tree Farm

Ainthorpe Rigg

Plum Tree Farm

Church

Trig Point

Danby Rigg

Earth Works

Bottom Grove

Danby Dale

East Cliff

uphill on to Danby Rigg.

From the top the view encompasses the whole of Danby Dale. The group of buildings to the south (left) is Botton Village; to the west is Castleton Rigg.

The path continues over the moor in a north-easterly direction. Initially, it is not very distinct but does become clearer, if only narrow, after a few yards, and passes to the left of two piles of stones. Maintain this course, through the heather, until its junction with a much broader path, then bear left along the eastern edge of the rigg. To the right is Little Fryup Dale and beyond, separated by Fairy Cross Plain, Great Fryup Dale. Continue in a northerly direction, taking care to ignore the path bearing left to the trig point, until reaching the junction with a path climbing on to the rigg from the road. Bear left to pass a broad, flat, standing stone, then continue downhill through the gate to the road. Turn left to regain Ainthorpe village.

N.B. The route along the eastern edge of Danby Rigg is not a definitive right of way, but is a path well used, apparently without objection, by many walkers.

Distance: 5 miles.

Glaisdale and Arnecliff Wood

Starting point: Arncliffe Arms, Glaisdale, G.R. 782054: the inn offers light refreshments only.

Glaisdale is a typical dales village, the valley areas being used for farming whilst the higher ridges are strewn with heather and bracken. Although now entirely rural, the area was once worked for ironstone. The earliest recorded smelting was in 1223, but the industry was at its height between 1868 and 1875. Terraces of miners houses are still occupied, whilst other visible remains include grass covered mounds, indicating old slag heaps, and piles for the original river bridge, close to the present bridge. This bridge was necessary to transport the ironstone, from the mine, to the blast furnaces. Three blast furnaces were operated, by the Cleveland Iron Company, when the industry was at its peak. They closed in 1876, but it was over 40 years before removal of the massive slag heaps was underetaken.

Beggars Bridge is one of numerous arched bridges, built during medieval times, to facilitate the safe passage of pack-horses across rivers. Characteristic of such bridges are the low outward leaning walls which allow easy access for the laden pack-horse. This particular bridge was rebuilt in 1619 and is linked with a legend of young lovers separated by the swollen River Esk. The paved track leading through Arncliff Wood, to the bridge, was also used by the pack-horse trains until approximately 200 years ago. The hollowed centre of the sandstone slabs is an indicator of many centuries' wear.

Route: From the inn car park turn right, on to the metalled road, then immediately right again on to the downhill footpath. Cross the beck by the footbridge, then bear right along the forest road. Continue ahead in a southerly direction until this road forks, at which point bear left to follow the track climbing the spur of the hill. This track eventually becomes enclosed by walls and should be followed until the first gate on the left is reached. Keep to the woodland path until the motor road is reached. Turn uphill for a few yards, then left, through a field gate. Follow the right-hand boundary of two fields, before joining the track leading through Butter Park Farm finally to reach Lodge Hill. After passing in front of the farmhouse continue through the left-hand gate, then bear

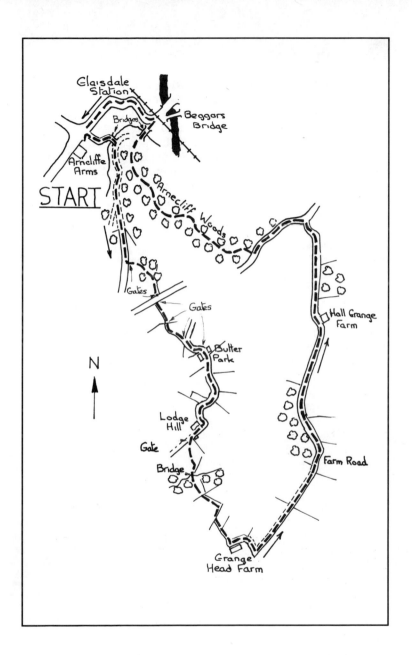

Glaisdale
Station

Beggars
Bridge

Bridges

Arncliffe
Arms

START

Arncliff Woods

Gates

Gates

Butter
Park

N

Hall Grange
Farm

Lodge
Hill

Gate

Bridge

Farm Road

Grange
Head Farm

diagonally downhill, across the field, to join a paved path. Cross the beck, then climb uphill before turning left along the top of the wood to pass through a field gate.

Follow the left-hand boundary of this field, as far as the gate opposite, then the right-hand boundary of two fields, to emerge at Grange Head Farm. From here, continue along the farm road until its junction with the motor road, a distance of approximately 1½ miles. Turn uphill for about a quarter mile, then take the right-hand path leading into Arnecliff Wood. Follow the paved path, which runs above, and alongside, the River Esk, until a flight of steps is reached. Descend the steps and pass under the railway arch to view Beggars Bridge. Having done so, retrace the route under the arch to follow the road back to the start.

Distance: 5 miles.

Roxby

Starting point: The Fox Inn, Roxby, G.R. 763159: the inn is residential and offers light refreshments.

Roxby is situated at the mid-point of a minor road linking the A171 and A174 Middlesbrough–Whitby roads. Its small population is centred around the church of St. Nicholas, which has Tudor origins but was extensively rebuilt in 1818. The nearest large village is Staithes, 2½ miles to the north-east.

Route: From the inn turn downhill, as far as a sharp right-hand bend. The view ahead encompasses Cleveland Potash Mine and beyond to the farmland topping Boulby Cliff. On the bend pass through a metal farm gate to follow a broad path towards Roxby Woods. Where the path forks, keep right to pass Low House and enter the woods by a stile in the field corner. Continue along the main path, then take the second fork downhill to the footbridge across Roxby Beck. Having crossed the beck proceed uphill to emerge on to Ridge Lane. Turn left along the lane for over half a mile, until reaching a signposted footpath on the right, which should be followed to Easington Beck. At this point the beck marks the boundary between modern Cleveland and North Yorkshire. Bear left up the occasionally stepped, bracken covered slope. Near the top the path passes between sycamore trees, before turning sharp right towards the hedge and over a plank footbridge.

Bear left along the field boundary and through the garden of Spring House Cottages to emerge on to a rough lane. Turn left to follow this lane through Grinkle Park Farm and out on to Grinkle Lane. Again, bear left, passing the entrance to Grinkle Park Hotel, until reaching a large double gate opening on to a wide, grassy path. Continue ahead to the top of the wood, and along the path leading down to the beck. Cross over by the stepping stones, then continue ahead, past a neglected farm, eventually reaching Ridge Lane adjacent to a water filter plant. Turn left along the lane, for approximately a mile, before turning right on to a signposted footpath towards Roxby Beck. Shortly after the path bears left, turn right, cross a stile and descend to the beck.

The path then continues uphill to emerge into rough pasture. Cross this pasture diagonally to the top left-hand corner, then

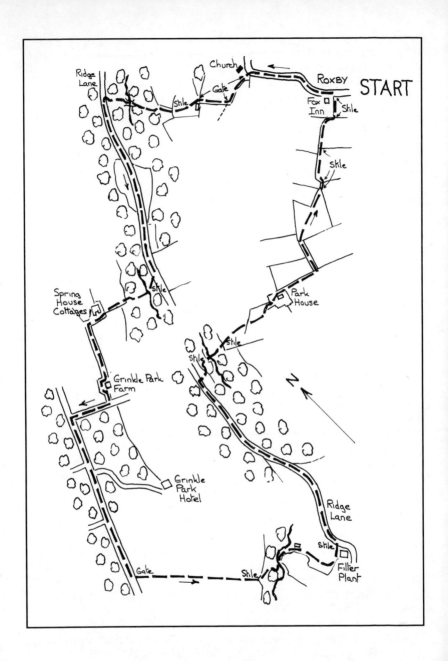

START

Roxby

Church

Gate

Shle

Ridge
Lane

Fox
Inn

Shle

Shle

Park
House

Shle

Shle

Spring
House
Cottages

Shle

Grinkle Park
Farm

N

Grinkle
Park
Hotel

Ridge
Lane

Shle

Filter
Plant

Gate

Shle

50

follow the distinct path to Park House. After joining the farm road keep left, alongside a fence, before turning sharp left into an enclosed green lane, which opens out to bear diagonally right across grazing pasture. The path then follows the left-hand boundary of four fields before returning to the start.

Distance: 6 miles.

Goldsborough and the Heritage Coast

Starting point: The Red Lion, Lythe, G.R. 846131: the inn is residential and offers light refreshments.

Goldsborough is a hamlet situated on the cliffs north-east of Lythe. In a field to the north, the site of a fourth century Roman signal station is clearly visible.

The Heritage Coasts are stretches of coastline identified as being the most attractive in England and Wales. Within ancient Cleveland the area now so designated would have run from Saltburn to beyond Lythe. It is a coastline dominated by steep cliffs, rising to a maximum height of 680 feet at Boulby. Other dramatic scenery has been created by the erosion and weathering of rock and clay and the crumbly nature of the strata. The stretch included in this walk has a very stoney platform and reveals signs of previous alum and jet mining. West of Kettleness the cliff-line retreats inland to form Runswick Bay. The coastline included in the Huntcliff–Saltburn walk is also part of this length of Heritage Coast.

Route: Follow the main road east, towards the church. Immediately past the police station go through a wooden gate, then cross the field to another gate in the bottom right-hand corner. Continue ahead, along the boundary, before entering an enclosed green lane leading to the top of the wood. The path descends to the beck, climbs up again, then bears left through a small gate to reach Overdale Farm. Pass to the left of the main buildings and out onto the farm road, which should be followed to the motor road. Turn right towards Goldsborough. In the hamlet keep ahead, then bear right through the farm on Whinney Hill. After passing through a gate continue diagonally left towards an old cottage. To the right the site of the Roman signal station is readily identifiable and affords extensive views of the coastline from Boulby to Whitby.

The route maintains its diagonal course, to rejoin the road beyond the Victorian chapel of St. John the Baptist. Continue towards the cliff top, then turn right on to the coastal footpath for approximately two miles. With Lythe church visible to the right, cross a stile bearing an acorn emblem, before turning along the field boundary to pass a low hillock on the left. Enter the wood by a stile in the field corner, descend the stepped path to the footbridge, then

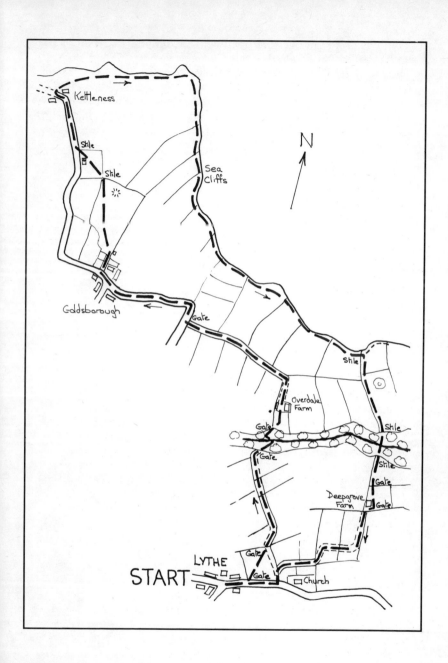

Kettleness

Sea Cliffs

N

Goldsborough

Gate

Stile

Overdale Farm

Gate

Stile

Gate

Stile

Gate

Deepgrove Farm

Gate

Gate

Gate

Gate

LYTHE

START

Church

climb again to emerge into open fields. Continue ahead along the hedge before bearing to the left of Deepgrove Farm, then right on to the access road. This should be followed to the main road to regain Lythe.

The access road passes St. Oswald's Church. Although almost entirely rebuilt in 1910, it dates back to around the thirteenth century. Remains of the old buildings are to be found in the present church.

Distance: 6 miles.